HOCKEY SUPERSTARS

Paul Romanuk

ALL-TIME GREATS!

VOL. 2

Scholastic Canada Ltd.

Toronto New York London Auckland Sydney
Mexico City New Delhi Hong Kong Buenos Aires

For every young player who picks up a stick
and dreams of being an all-time great.

Acknowledgements and references: The author would like to acknowledge
several outstanding sources of information used in compiling this book:
legendsofhockey.net, NHL.com, canadiens.nhl.com, redwings.nhl.com,
torontomapleleafs.nhl.com, *Total NHL* (Dan Diamond & Associates, 2003),
Total Hockey, 2nd Edition (Total Sports Publishing, 2000), and *NHL 75th
Anniversary Commemorative Book* (McClelland & Stewart Ltd., 1991).

Cover: Bruce Bennett/Getty Images
Bobby Clarke, Marcel Dionne, Larry Robinson, Borje Salming, Stan Mikita:
Portnoy/Hockey Hall of Fame
Bernie Geoffrion: Michael Burns Sr./Hockey Hall of Fame
Glenn Hall, Red Kelly, Ted Lindsay, Frank Mahovlich, Terry Sawchuk: Imperial Oil/Turofsky
Hockey Hall of Fame
Brett Hull: Dave Sanford/Hockey Hall of Fame
Jari Kurri: Paul Bereswill/Hockey Hall of Fame
Mark Messier, Peter Stastny:, Bryan Trottier: O-Pee-Chee/Hockey Hall of Fame
Henri Richard (left): Imperial Oil/Turofsky/Hockey Hall of Fame;
(right) Portnoy/Hockey Hall of Fame
Eddie Shore (left): Le Studio du Hockey/Hockey Hall of Fame; (right) Hockey Hall of Fame
Georges Vezina: Hockey Hall of Fame
Steve Yzerman: David E. Klutho
Ted Lindsay Award: Steve Poirier/Hockey Hall of Fame
All other awards: Doug MacLellan/Hockey Hall of Fame

Library and Archives Canada Cataloguing in Publication
Romanuk, Paul
Hockey superstars : all-time greats! / Paul Romanuk.
ISBN 978-1-4431-0736-5 (v. 1).--ISBN 978-1-4431-0712-9 (v. 2)
1. Hockey players--Biography--Juvenile literature. 2. National
Hockey League--Biography--Juvenile literature. I. Title.
GV848.5.A1R652 2011   j796.962092'2   C2011-902076-9

6 5 4 3 2 1   Printed in Canada 118   11 12 13 14 15

MIX
Paper from
responsible sources
FSC® C011825
FSC
www.fsc.org

INTRODUCTION

This is a picture of me that was taken by my mother when I was 13 years old. I'm in my bedroom, where the walls were plastered with pictures of hockey players I'd cut out of newspapers and magazines. Some of the players in *All-Time Greats! Volume 2* were playing back when that photo was taken. Researching them for this book and *All Time Greats! Volume 1*, brought back many happy memories of sitting with my best friend, Tim, and watching guys like Frank Mahovlich, Borje Salming, Larry Robinson and Bryan Trottier when they were at their best. After we watched them play, we'd head out to the driveway to take shots and pretend to be one of those greats.

I'm a lot older now, and I don't have pictures of players on my bedroom walls, but I still love the game. I don't think that will ever go away (unlike my hair).

BOBBY CLARKE

Bobby Clarke was a fantastic junior player with the Flin Flon Bombers in the Western Canada Junior Hockey League. He led the league in scoring three years in a row and was considered by scouts to be an extremely hard-working player. But because he was diabetic, many wondered if he would be able to endure the rigors of the NHL. They couldn't have been more wrong.

So instead of being a high pick in the 1969 NHL Amateur Draft, he went 17th overall. It turned out to be one of the best picks the Philadelphia Flyers ever made. Bobby earned himself a spot on the team in his first season and went on to become the symbol of the franchise during a brilliant 15-season career.

> **"I've never seen anybody put the feeling into words properly. We all felt the same way, whether you won it in Montreal or Toronto or in Philadelphia. When you win the Stanley Cup after dreaming about it your whole life, for me, it was the highlight of my hockey playing career."**

A turning point in Bobby's career came in the famous Canada–Soviet Union Summit Series in 1972. He was one of the best players on the team. He carried that experience back to the NHL and had his best season yet. He was named the Hart Trophy winner as the league's Most Valuable Player after becoming the first expansion team player to score more than 100 points in a season (37 goals, 67 assists, for 104 points).

"Playing in that series did a lot for my confidence," recalls Bobby. "You find out that you can play at a different level . . . I think it advanced my career by two or three years."

In 1973–1974 Bobby led the Flyers to the first of his two Stanley Cup Championships. Philadelphia played an aggressive game and became known as the "Broad Street Bullies." Bobby was well known among fellow NHL players as a guy who would do anything to win, and that included using his stick to slash and hack in front of the net. Today, that wouldn't be tolerated, but back then it was something that most players thought of as a part of the game, for better or worse.

Bobby retired after the 1983–1984 season and was almost immediately named the Flyers' general manager. He left for brief periods to work as a general manager for the Minnesota North Stars and the Florida Panthers, but he always returned to Philadelphia.

Bobby was welcomed into the Hockey Hall of Fame in 1987.

Did You Know?

Bobby's junior hockey coach took him to the famous Mayo Clinic in the United States and had doctors provide a letter saying that Bobby could play professional hockey as long as he took care of his health. The coach then showed that to any scouts who watched Bobby play.

Totals 1969–1970 to 1983–1984

	GP	G	A	PTS	PIM
Regular Season	1144	358	852	1210	1453
Playoffs	136	42	77	119	152

Born: August 13, 1949, in Flin Flon, Manitoba
Position: Center
Height: 1.78 m (5'10")
Weight: 84 kg (185 lbs.)
NHL Teams: Philadelphia Flyers

CAREER STATS

Major Awards Stanley Cup: 1974, 1975
Hart Memorial Trophy: 1973, 1975, 1976
Lester B. Pearson Award: 1973
Bill Masterton Memorial Trophy: 1972
Frank J. Selke Trophy: 1983
Lester Patrick Trophy: 1980

MARCEL DIONNE

Marcel Dionne was a great player who never got a chance to play for a great team. Marcel played most of his career for the struggling Los Angeles Kings. Despite that, he became one of the NHL's offensive superstars. He topped the 100-point mark, finished in the NHL top ten scorers seven times and won the scoring title in 1979–1980. When he retired in 1988–1989, only legends Gordie Howe and Wayne Gretzky had more career points than the "Little Beaver" from Drummondville, Quebec.

"In Los Angeles, once you leave the parking lot of the arena you're invisible. A lot of guys liked that. I didn't. I like the heat to be on and have people aware of the team."

Marcel was drafted second overall by the Detroit Red Wings in the 1971 Amateur Draft, after the Montreal Canadiens took Guy Lafleur. He had four very good seasons with Detroit, including a 121-point season in 1974–1975. However, he wanted out of Detroit and forced the team to trade him to the Los Angeles Kings.

"Going to L.A. was a new beginning for me," Marcel recalled years later. "The travel was tough and we had trouble finding time to practice because of all the travel, but it was still a great place to play."

Marcel finished as the Kings' all-time scoring leader with 1,307 points (550 goals and 757 assists) in almost 12 seasons. He also holds the club's "Ironman" record for most consecutive games played after he appeared in 324 games. Late in the 1986–1987 season, he was traded to the New York Rangers. In 1987–1988, his last full season in the NHL, Marcel managed 65 points. He played 37 games the following season and knew the time had come to retire.

Internationally, Marcel played for Canada in two Canada Cups and four World Championships. He was also on the Canadian team that won the 1972 Summit Series against the Soviet Union. Although he never dressed for a game, he describes being part of the 1972 team as "the greatest experience of my career, by far." He also played in the first Canada Cup tournament in 1976 alongside fellow future Hall of Famers Bobby Hull and Phil Esposito. And, during overtime in the deciding game against Czechoslovakia, while on a line with Darryl Sittler and Lanny McDonald, he got an assist on Sittler's tournament-winning goal.

The Little Beaver was inducted into the Hockey Hall of Fame in 1992.

Did You Know?

The highest scoring French-Canadian player of all-time isn't Mario Lemieux or Luc Robitaille or Guy Lafleur — it is none other than Marcel Dionne.

Born: August 3, 1951, in Drummondville, Quebec
Position: Center
Height: 1.75 m (5'9")
Weight: 86 kg (190 lbs.)
NHL Teams: Detroit Red Wings, Los Angeles Kings, New York Rangers

CAREER STATS

Totals 1971–1972 to 1988–1989

	GP	G	A	PTS	PIM
Regular Season	1348	731	1040	1771	600
Playoffs	49	21	24	45	17

Major Awards   Art Ross Trophy: 1980
Lady Byng Memorial Trophy: 1975, 1977
Lester B. Pearson Award: 1979, 1980

BERNIE GEOFFRION

No player was was as determined and hard working as Bernie Geoffrion. His determination to win was legendary, and when he was on a roll, there weren't many players better than "Boom Boom."

Boom Boom grew up in Montreal and dreamed of playing for the Canadiens. His dream came true when the Habs signed him and he pulled on the famed *bleu, blanc et rouge* for the first time on December 16, 1950. That night he found himself sitting in the same dressing room as his hockey hero, the great Maurice "Rocket" Richard.

"I always did have the confidence. When someone would score two goals, I'd say to myself, 'I'm gonna get three.'"

"I told The Rocket that I knew I'd never be able to reach his level, but he was the guy I wanted to be like. I always thought that if I was going to be like somebody, the Rocket was the guy."

So it was remarkable that, five years later, he was battling his boyhood hero for the NHL scoring title. Although The Rocket was a brilliant player, he had never reached that goal. But late in the season, The Rocket hit a referee and was suspended. That opened the door for Boom Boom to pass his teammate and win the title. Years later it was revealed that he had planned to ease off so he wouldn't pass Richard, but several players had told him that it wouldn't be right. So Boom Boom went on to win the scoring title. Some Montreal fans felt that he had robbed Richard of his first Art Ross Trophy. But they would later cheer him on as one of the greatest players on an amazing team that went on to win five consecutive Stanley Cup Championships, from 1955–1956 through 1959–1960, something that had never been done before. In 1960–1961 Boom Boom had his best season ever, winning his second scoring title and also becoming only the second player in NHL history to score 50 goals in a season (Richard was the first).

Boom Boom announced his retirement after the 1963–1964 season, and coached in Montreal's minor league system. But after two seasons, he returned to the NHL and played two more seasons with the New York Rangers. He retired for good in 1968 and returned to coaching. He coached 281 games in the NHL for three different teams between 1968 and 1980 — including 30 for his beloved Montreal Canadiens.

Boom Boom was inducted into the Hockey Hall of Fame in 1972. He passed away on March 11, 2006.

Did You Know?

Many credit Boom Boom with inventing the slapshot. He was given his nickname by a Montreal newspaper reporter back when he was playing junior hockey. It came from the sound the puck made leaving his stick — boom! — and hitting the boards — boom! — as he practised his shot.

Born: February 16, 1931, in Montreal, Quebec

Position: Right Wing

Height: 1.75 m (5'9")

Weight: 75 kg (166 lbs.)

NHL Teams: Montreal Canadiens, New York Rangers

CAREER STATS

Totals 1950–1951 to 1967–1968

	GP	G	A	PTS	PIM
Regular Season	883	393	429	822	689
Playoffs	132	58	60	118	88
Major Awards	Stanley Cup: 1953, 1956, 1957, 1958, 1959, 1960				
	Calder Memorial Trophy: 1952				
	Art Ross Trophy: 1955, 1961				
	Hart Memorial Trophy: 1961				

GLENN HALL

Being a goalie, in any sport, is often described as the loneliest position on the team. So it makes sense that a man who has said in interviews over the years that he's "quite comfortable being alone," was one of the greatest goalies of all time.

Playing behind some good teams and a few great ones, Glenn Hall's career spanned 18 seasons. He appeared in over 900 NHL regular season games and 115 playoff games and became known as "Mr. Goalie." During one stretch, Glenn played an amazing 502 consecutive regular season games. The streak started at the beginning of the 1955–1956 season with the Detroit Red Wings and finished 13 games into the 1962–1963 season, with the Chicago Blackhawks. He was the NHL Rookie of the Year, a Vezina Trophy winner and also a Stanley Cup champion during his amazing run.

"Goaltenders are a breed apart; Glenn Hall is apart from that breed."

—Hall of Fame coach Scotty Bowman

Glenn also created the butterfly style of goaltending. That's where the goalie drops to his knees and spreads, or "butterflies" his pads out along the ice to cover the bottom part of the net. Like many great inventions, Glenn came upon the style because he had to.

"I had a groin injury at the time," he said, "and found that you could work around doing the split [a move where the goalie spreads his legs quickly to cover both corners of the net] if you got into the butterfly."

Glenn was ready to retire after the 1966–1967 season, when the NHL expanded from six to twelve teams. He was claimed in the Expansion Draft by St. Louis and played another four seasons with the Blues. The team had a great blend of young players and veterans like Glenn, as well as a talented young coach, Scotty Bowman. That combination got the team to the Stanley Cup Final three years in a row, although they never won a Cup.

After he retired, Mr. Goalie worked with a few teams over the years as a goaltending coach and consultant. He was elected to the Hockey Hall of Fame in 1973.

Did You Know?

Glenn often didn't feel as though he was ready for a game unless he was throwing up beforehand. The condition became known in the hockey world as "having a Glenn Hall stomach."

Born: October 3, 1931, in
Humboldt, Saskatchewan
Position: Goaltender
Height: 1.80 m (5'11")
Weight: 82 kg (180 lbs.)
NHL Teams: Detroit Red Wings,
Chicago Blackhawks, St. Louis Blues

CAREER STATS

Totals 1952–1953 to 1970–1971

	GP	W	L	T	SO	GAA
Regular Season	906	407	326	163	84	2.49
Playoffs	115	49	65	--	6	2.78

Major Awards   Stanley Cup: 1961
Calder Memorial Trophy: 1956
Conn Smythe Trophy: 1968
Vezina Trophy: 1963, 1967, 1969

When do four letters feel like the weight of the world on a young NHL player's shoulders? When those letters are H-U-L-L and you're the son of a hockey legend.

"Knowing how great he was, it was natural growing up to want to be that good or even to surpass what he had done," said Brett about his legendary father, Bobby Hull.

"You gave me the best advice that you ever could have given: 'The further you are from the play, the closest you are to it,' and I'm really fortunate that I was able to figure out what the heck you were talking about."

—During his Hockey Hall of Fame induction speech, Brett Hull jokes about fatherly advice from Bobby Hull.

Brett has admitted that he was a "late bloomer" in hockey. He almost quit the game when he was 18 years old and couldn't find a team that wanted him. The following year, a friend who was going to try out for a team urged him to give it another shot. He eventually earned a spot on the Penticton Knights in the British Columbia Junior Hockey League.

Brett was drafted by the Calgary Flames as the 117th overall pick in 1984, then spent two seasons playing at the University of Minnesota Duluth before debuting with the Flames. He played five games with Calgary in 1986–1987, and earned a regular spot on the Flames the next season. However, he didn't play for Calgary very long. Brett was traded, along with a teammate, to the St. Louis Blues late that season.

In his first full season with St. Louis, Brett led the team in scoring with 84 points. But it was the following season when the "The Golden Brett" (a nickname given to him as a tribute to his father, "The Golden Jet") blasted his way to superstar status, leading the league with 72 goals. He led the league in goal-scoring for the next three seasons. In 1990–1991 he hit his career high of 86 goals and was named the winner of both the Hart Trophy and the Lester B. Pearson Award.

Brett spent 10 seasons with the Blues and is the all-time franchise goal-scoring leader (527 goals). He left St. Louis and signed as a free agent with the Dallas Stars, where he was part of his first Stanley Cup Championship in 1999. He signed as a free agent with Detroit in 2001–2002 and won a Cup with the Red Wings in 2002 as part of what he later recalled as "maybe the greatest team ever assembled." Brett signed as a free agent with Phoenix in 2004, but the season was cancelled because of the lockout. After just five games in 2005–2006, he called it quits for good.

Did You Know?

Brett and his father Bobby are the only father and son team in NHL history to have each scored 600 career goals, recorded more than 1,000 career points, and won the Hart Trophy.

Born: August 9, 1964, in Belleville, Ontario

Position: Center

Height: 1.80 m (5'11")

Weight: 91 kg (200 lbs.)

NHL Teams: Calgary Flames, St. Louis Blues, Detroit Red Wings, Dallas Stars, Phoenix Coyotes

CAREER STATS

Totals 1985–1986 to 2005–2006

	GP	G	A	PTS	PIM
Regular Season	1269	741	650	1391	458
Playoffs	202	103	87	190	73

Major Awards	
	Stanley Cup: 1999, 2002
	Hart Memorial Trophy: 1991
	Lady Byng Memorial Trophy: 1990
	Lester B. Pearson Award: 1991

RED KELLY

Red Kelly was an amazing hockey player for many reasons: his ability to control the pace of play, his excellent passing ability and unselfishness with the puck, and his strength. On top of all that, Red was also one of the best of his era both as a defenseman and a center — something that has never been done since.

"What more can you ask [for] in life, than playing the game that you love to play, and it's your living? It was a great way to go through life."

After playing forward as a junior, Red started his career as a defenseman with the Detroit Red Wings in 1947–1948. He impressed both his teammates and coaches because of his great attitude and his ability to quickly adapt from junior hockey to the NHL level. By his third season in the league he was one of the top players at his position. Starting in 1949–1950, he was named to the NHL First or Second All-Star Team for eight consecutive seasons (six First All-Star Team selections and two Second Team). In 1954 Red received the first James Norris Trophy as the NHL's top defenseman. Along with all of the individual praise, Red was also a part of four Stanley Cup Championships with the Red Wings.

Red's career in Detroit came to a strange end. During the 1959–1960 season he played with a broken bone in one of his feet. The injury was a secret to the public. But when people criticized him for his unimpressive play, management didn't defend him and even traded him to the New York Rangers. Red was disgusted by the treatment from his long-time club and announced his retirement. As a result, the NHL voided the trade. But Toronto Maple Leafs general manager Punch Imlach arranged a trade for Red's rights from Detroit. Imlach then talked the veteran into coming out of retirement to play for the Leafs. It was a dream come true for Red, who had grown up always wanting to play for the Leafs. But, once in Toronto, Imlach decided that he would use Red as a centerman, not a defenseman. He felt that Red would match up well against Jean Béliveau, the great Canadiens centerman. And Imlach was right, as Red settled in playing on a line with Frank Mahovlich that helped lead the Leafs to three straight Cup titles. Red went out in style, retiring after the Leafs' Stanley Cup Championship in 1967. He went on to coach a total of 742 regular season games in Los Angeles, Pittsburgh and then Toronto. Red became a member of the Hockey Hall of Fame in 1969.

Did You Know?

Aside from being a defenseman, a forward and later, a coach, Red was also a Canadian Member of Parliament. He served three years as an MP (1962 to 1964) while he was playing for the Leafs. He would commute between Toronto and Ottawa in between games.

Born: July 9, 1927, in
Simcoe, Ontario
Position: Defense/Center
Height: 1.80 m (5'11")
Weight: 82 kg (180 lbs.)
NHL Teams: Detroit Red
Wings, Toronto Maple
Leafs

Totals 1947–1948 to 1966–1967

	GP	G	A	PTS	PIM
Regular Season	1316	281	542	823	327
Playoffs	164	33	59	92	51

Major Awards Stanley Cup Championship: 1950, 1952, 1954,
1955, 1962, 1963, 1964, 1967
Lady Byng Memorial Trophy: 1951, 1953, 1954, 1961
James Norris Memorial Trophy: 1954

JARI KURRI

Back in 1980, Jari Kurri didn't think he'd be in North America playing in the NHL for very long.

"I remember thinking that I'd give it one year," recalls Jari. "I had tough times in my first year . . . being away from the old country, my parents and friends. It's not just the hockey that's different but a whole different lifestyle."

Jari stayed longer than a year, of course, and went on to become one of the greatest players in NHL history. He was part of five Stanley Cup Championships with the Edmonton Oilers' dynasty during the 1980s. Jari finished his career as the highest-scoring European-born and -trained player in NHL history with 1,398 career points (he has since been passed by Jaromir Jagr).

> **"I didn't know how big a deal the Cup was until I saw the effect that it had on my teammates, the fans and other players. That made me realize how important it was and what a great achievement it was. Winning that first Cup was my biggest thrill."**

Many of the points that Jari tallied came while playing right wing for the Oilers on a line with the man most consider to be the greatest player ever — Wayne Gretzky. Gretzky and Jari became linemates about three months into the 1980–1981 season . . . and it was magic. Their run together in Edmonton lasted eight seasons and featured four Stanley Cup Championships. The two were reunited in Los Angeles, where they played on the same line again from 1991–1992 until Gretzky was traded late in the 1995–1996 season.

After almost five seasons in Los Angeles, Jari was traded to the New York Rangers where injuries held him to only 14 games. He then signed on as a free agent for one season with the Mighty Ducks of Anaheim, where he played with fellow Finnish legend Teemu Selanne. Jari moved on to Colorado to play one final season before announcing his retirement.

On the international stage, Jari played in four World Championships with the Finnish Lions. He also played in three Canada Cup tournaments and one World Cup. During his final NHL season, he represented Finland in the 1998 Nagano Winter Olympics where the Finns won a bronze medal. He is widely considered the greatest Finnish hockey player ever — pretty impressive for a guy who didn't expect to last more than a season in the NHL.

Did You Know?

Jari played more games with Gretzky (858) and assisted on more of his goals (196) than anyone else.

Born: May 18, 1960, in Helsinki, Finland

Position: Right Wing

Height: 1.85 m (6'1")

Weight: 88 kg (195 lbs.)

NHL Teams: Edmonton Oilers, Los Angeles Kings, New York Rangers, Mighty Ducks of Anaheim, Colorado Avalanche

CAREER STATS

Totals 1980–1981 to 1997–1998

	GP	G	A	PTS	PIM
Regular Season	1251	601	797	1398	545
Playoffs	200	106	127	233	123
Major Awards	Stanley Cup: 1984, 1985, 1987, 1988, 1990				
	Lady Byng Memorial Trophy: 1985				

TED LINDSAY

Ted Lindsay was one of the meanest, toughest players in the history of the game, and he was also one of the best left-wingers ever to lace on a pair of skates.

"Terrible Ted" was pretty small for an NHL player, but because he was known as a guy who never backed down, he was feared. You could try to elbow him, and he'd elbow you right back. If you tried to put him off his game with a slash, he'd slash you right back, twice as hard.

"The two-year contract I signed ended up being 17 years over 21 years . . . and the greatest life in the world. I'm envious of all the young guys playing today who have all this to look forward to. It's just a wonderful life."

But there was more to Ted than just toughness: he played left wing on one of the great lines in NHL history — "The Production Line." His linemates were Gordie Howe and Sid Abel and together, they helped lead the Red Wings during a spectacular run from 1948–1949 through 1954–1955. During that time, Detroit finished in first place seven seasons in a row and won the Stanley Cup four times. Howe won the scoring title four times and Ted won it once (1949–1950, when the Production Line finished 1-2-3 in the scoring race: Lindsay–Abel–Howe).

Ted was also one of the first NHL players to realize that the owners weren't giving the players a fair deal. At that time, players were underpaid and kept in the dark about their pensions and other off-ice issues. Ted tried to form a players association to try to work with the owners on some of those issues. But the owners weren't happy about that and threatened the players involved with the planning, even trading some of them. Not even Ted was safe. Despite 13 seasons with the Red Wings and coming off the best season of his career (85 points), Ted was traded to the last-place Chicago Blackhawks. He later said that the attempt to put together a player's association had "changed my life, changed my career and changed my stats."

Ted played three seasons for the Blackhawks and helped them go from one of the worst teams in the league to a Stanley Cup contender. He retired after the 1959–1960 season but came out of retirement four seasons later and played one final season with his beloved Detroit Red Wings. In retirement, Ted worked as Detroit's general manager from 1976 until 1980. He also coached the team for 29 games, in the 1979–1980 season and the 1980–1981 season.

Ted was inducted into the Hockey Hall of Fame in 1966.

Did You Know?

In 1955, when Ted accepted the Stanley Cup as captain of the Red Wings, he lifted it over his head and took it for a victory lap around the ice. Ted was the first captain ever to do this and it is a tradition that has carried on to this day.

Born: July 29, 1925, in Renfrew, Ontario

Position: Left Wing

Height: 1.73 m (5'8")

Weight: 74 kg (163 lbs.)

NHL Teams: Detroit Red Wings, Chicago Blackhawks

CAREER STATS

Totals 1944–1945 to 1964–1965

	GP	G	A	PTS	PIM
Regular Season	1068	379	472	851	1808
Playoffs	133	47	49	96	194
Major Awards	Stanley Cup: 1950, 1952, 1954, 1955				
	Art Ross Trophy: 1950				

FRANK MAHOVLICH

Frank Mahovlich was a great junior player with the St. Mike's Majors. Both his size and booming shot had people expecting that he would dominate in the NHL after a few years of experience. And after he beat out Bobby Hull to win the Calder Trophy as the Rookie of the Year in 1957, people were sure of it. However, it seemed that no matter how hard he tried and how well he played, it was never enough for demanding Toronto hockey fans and, in particular, Toronto's successful, but hard, coach Punch Imlach. The stress took its toll on Frank. He and Imlach barely spoke to one another for five years and Frank was treated a couple of times for severe depression.

> **"I gave it my best shot; I think I always went to the wall, and I'm quite proud of what I achieved."**

Still, "The Big M" was one of the Leafs' best players — leading the team in scoring every season from 1960–1961 until 1965–1966. During that time he topped the 30-goal mark four times, including a 48-goal season in 1960–1961. That was at a time when only a handful of players would score 30 goals in a season, and 50 was almost unheard of. Frank was also part of four Stanley Cup Championships with the Leafs.

Things improved for Frank when he was traded to the Detroit Red Wings near the end of the 1967–1968 season. Away from Imlach and the pressure in Toronto, he enjoyed two great seasons in Detroit, twice hitting the 70-point mark. The Big M was traded to the Montreal Canadiens at the 1971 trade deadline, and he went on to help the Habs win the Cup that spring and again in 1972–1973 (recording his 1,000th career point along the way).

After the 1973–1974 season, Frank, then 36 years old, signed a lucrative deal to play for the Toronto Toros in the World Hockey Association. He played four years in that league before heading back to the NHL to try to earn a spot with Detroit. But during training camp, Frank knew he'd had enough. He left camp and, a few days later, announced his retirement.

Frank was inducted into the Hockey Hall of Fame in 1981. He also received another honor in 1998 when he became the first former hockey player to be appointed to Canada's Senate by Prime Minister Jean Chrétien. It was a fitting appointment for a man who exuded class and grace under pressure during his 22 years as a professional hockey player.

Did You Know?

When the Montreal Canadiens first picked up Frank in a trade with Detroit, they didn't have a jersey ready with his number 27 on it. He had to play the first few games wearing number 10.

Born: January 10, 1938, in Timmins, Ontario
Position: Center
Height: 1.83 m (6')
Weight: 93 kg (205 lbs.)
NHL Teams: Toronto Maple Leafs, Detroit Red Wings, Montreal Canadiens

CAREER STATS

Totals 1956–1957 to 1973–1974

	GP	G	A	PTS	PIM
Regular Season	1181	533	570	1103	1056
Playoffs	137	51	67	118	163
Major Awards	Stanley Cup: 1962, 1963, 1964, 1967, 1971, 1973				
	Calder Memorial Trophy: 1958				

MARK MESSIER

Mark Messier was a tough player. "The Moose" was as respected for his ability to punish an opponent with a fierce bodycheck as he was for his ability to score big goals. Many old-timers liked to compare Mark to a legend from a different era, Gordie Howe, who enjoyed a similar reputation. So, it was one of the great honors of Mark's career when he passed Howe on the all-time NHL point-scoring list.

"Gordie's 'Mr. Hockey' . . . " said Mark back when he was about to pass Howe. "If you want to compare me to Gordie, I'll take it gladly."

"Individual statistics — goals and assists — weren't of interest to me. Figuring out a way to win in every individual game was what mattered."

Mark ended up with 1,887 career points (694 goals and 1,193 assists) — second on the all-time list, just behind his former teammate Wayne Gretzky.

Although his career point total was a big achievement, most people talk about his ability be a leader on almost every team he suited up for. According to many, Mark was one of the sport's greatest leaders.

Mark was already a team leader when he won the first of six Stanley Cups in 1984 with a brilliant young Edmonton Oilers team. He was also named the Conn Smythe Trophy winner that year. Mark went on to win four more Cups with the Oilers and another with the New York

Rangers during his 25-season career. He announced his retirement on September 12, 2005.

Part of Mark's legacy is an NHL award named after him: the Mark Messier Leadership Award. The award was introduced in 2006–2007 and is presented to recognize "great leadership qualities to his team, on and off the ice during the regular season."

Mark was inducted into the Hockey Hall of Fame in 2007.

"It's never about the individual making it to the Hall of Fame," said Mark during his induction speech. "It's about your minor hockey league coaches, your family, your friends and teammates along the way. You don't play team sports as an individual, you play with other people as a team."

That is a big part of what made Mark great. For all of his individual success, to Mark, it was always about the success of the group.

Did You Know?

Mark is the only player in the history of the NHL to captain two franchises to a Stanley Cup Championship. He did it with the Edmonton Oilers and the New York Rangers.

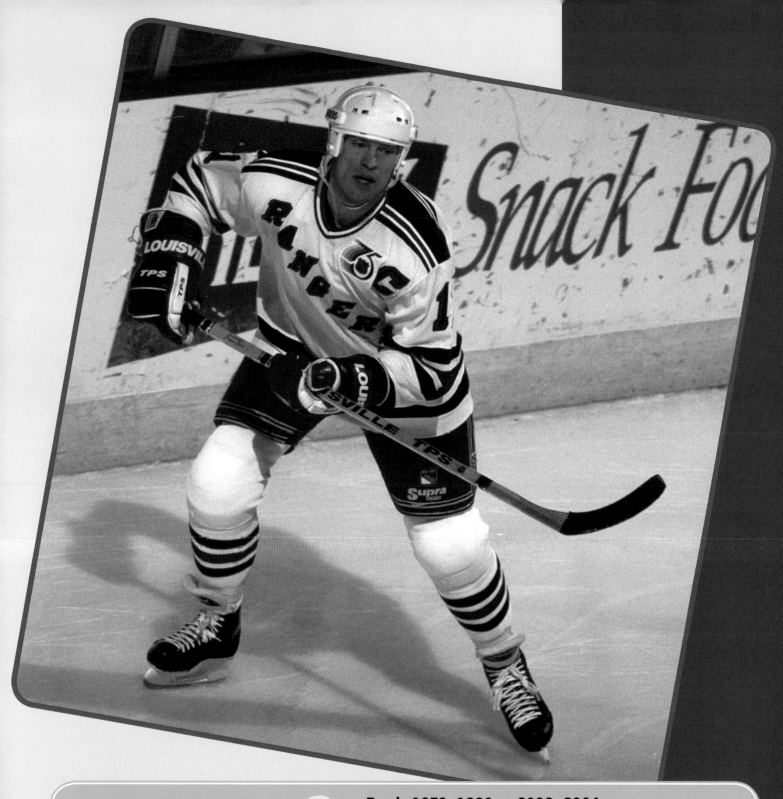

Born: January 18, 1961, in Edmonton, Alberta
Position: Left Wing/Center
Height: 1.85 m (6'1")
Weight: 93 kg (205 lbs.)
NHL Teams: Edmonton Oilers, New York Rangers, Vancouver Canucks

CAREER STATS

Totals 1979–1980 to 2003–2004

	GP	G	A	PTS	PIM
Regular Season	1756	694	1193	1887	1910
Playoffs	236	109	186	295	244
Major Awards	Stanley Cup: 1984, 1985, 1987, 1988, 1990, 1994				
	Conn Smythe Trophy: 1984				
	Hart Memorial Trophy: 1990, 1992				
	Lester B. Pearson Award: 1990, 1992				

STAN MIKITA

Stan Mikita was a giant of the game. He played 21 seasons with the Chicago Blackhawks, winning the Stanley Cup, scoring titles, and Most Valuable Player awards and made the change from being a player who had a reputation as someone who couldn't control his temper on the ice to being recognized as one of the game's gentlemen.

> **"My father told me when I left to go to Canada: 'Whatever you do, try to do it your best. Some days it's not going to be worth much, but at least you gave it your best shot.' And I've tried to follow that philosophy."**

In 1948 Stan left Czechoslovakia after his parents decided that he would have a much better life growing up in Canada. They arranged for him to be adopted by his aunt and uncle in St. Catharines, Ontario. Once there, Stan saw his first hockey game and wanted to give it a try. He was a natural and gained a reputation as a very good local player. Scouts for the Chicago Blackhawks heard about the young "foreign" player and liked what they saw. They signed him, and he eventually ended up playing for their junior team, the St. Catharines Teepees. When he was 18 years old, he was called up to Chicago for the 1959–1960 season. He recalls his first NHL faceoff against Montreal legend Jean Béliveau.

"I got to the faceoff circle and I looked up to see who I was facing, and I just kept looking up . . . and up! It was Béliveau! That was my first impression of hockey in Chicago."

In Stan's second season, he tallied 53 points, and then led the Hawks with six goals in the playoffs as the team won the Stanley Cup. Stan became one of the great playmakers in the game, winning the NHL scoring title four times in five seasons. In 1967 Stan became the first NHL player to win three major awards in the same season: the Art Ross Trophy as the league scoring leader, the Hart Trophy as the Most Valuable Player, and the Lady Byng Trophy as the most gentlemanly player. He then repeated the feat the following season. Although he had high penalty minutes early in his career, he had stopped taking "lazy penalties."

"It takes a pretty long stick to score from the penalty box," Stan said.

After back surgery in 1979, Stan knew it was time to bring his playing career to a close. Stan remains Chicago's all-time leader in points, assists and games played. He was welcomed into the Hall of Fame, alongside his long-time teammate and friend Bobby Hull, in 1983.

Did You Know?

Stan was one of the first players to discover the curved stick. The blade on a stick he was using during practice cracked. He noticed that when he fired the puck "it was a different feeling of the puck leaving the stick than I had ever felt" and that the puck moved erratically.

Born: May 20, 1940, in Sokolce, Czechoslovakia (now Slovakia)

Position: Center

Height: 1.75 m (5'9")

Weight: 77 kg (169 lbs.)

NHL Teams: Chicago Blackhawks

CAREER STATS

Totals 1958–1959 to 1979–1980

	GP	G	A	PTS	PIM
Regular Season	1394	541	926	1467	1270
Playoffs	155	59	91	150	169
Major Awards	Art Ross Trophy: 1964, 1965, 1967, 1968				
	Hart Memorial Trophy: 1967, 1968				
	Lady Byng Memorial Trophy: 1967, 1968				
	Lester Patrick Trophy: 1976				

HENRI RICHARD

The number that looms largest when looking at the amazing career of Henri "Pocket Rocket" Richard is 11 — 11 Stanley Cups.

Henri gained the nickname the "Pocket Rocket" because he is the younger and smaller brother of one of the giants of the game, Maurice "Rocket" Richard. When Henri joined the Montreal Canadiens for the 1955–1956 season, his older brother had already won championships and goal-scoring titles during a career that went back to 1942. It was a big shadow to try to emerge from. Many wondered how long the smaller, younger brother of a legend would last in the NHL. Montreal coach Toe Blake said at the time: "I had no plans for the kid, but every time you looked up during training camp, he had the puck on his stick and no one could take it away from him."

"I think that if you were to measure a man's heart, Henri would have been about ten foot six."

—Hall of Fame defenseman and former teammate Larry Robinson

Then, at a time when there were only six teams in the entire league, 19-year-old Henri emerged from the shadow of his legendary brother and made the team.

"A lot of people told me that playing with Maurice would add a lot of pressure, but I never felt any pressure," Henri said many years later. "My hero was my brother Maurice, and I wanted to do exactly like he did."

There was a 15-year age difference between the two brothers and, near the end of his great career, the Rocket said that playing with Henri gave him inspiration to want to keep playing. The two ended up skating together for five seasons — sometimes on the same line. In the end, although not as iconic as his older brother, Henri played more games, scored more points and was a part of more Stanley Cup Championships than the fabled Rocket.

Henri's career spanned two great eras in the Canadiens' history. The season he joined the team marked the first of five consecutive Stanley Cup Championships for the Habs. He continued to play through the 1960s and into the 1970s, when Montreal won another five Cups over the course of seven seasons. After he retired, he would often put his success down to being "in the right place at the right time," but anyone who saw Henri play saw a man with the heart of a lion who always tried to find a way to win.

Henri retired after the 1975 playoffs, at the end of a 20-season career. He was enshrined as a member of the Hockey Hall of Fame in 1979. His plaque in the Hall is right beside his brother's.

Did You Know?

Henri is one of only a handful of players who have scored a Stanley Cup-winning goal twice: in 1966, in overtime against Detroit, and in 1971 in Game 7 against Chicago.

Born: February 29, 1936, in Montreal, Quebec
Position: Center
Height: 1.70 m (5'7")
Weight: 73 kg (160 lbs.)
NHL Teams: Montreal Canadiens

CAREER STATS

Totals 1955–1956 to 1974–1975

	GP	G	A	PTS	PIM
Regular Season	1256	358	688	1046	928
Playoffs	180	49	80	129	181
Major Awards	Stanley Cup: 1956, 1957, 1958, 1959, 1960, 1965, 1966, 1968, 1969, 1971, 1973				
	Bill Masterton Memorial Trophy: 1974				

Larry Robinson has said that his first thought after he was drafted by the Montreal Canadiens in 1971 was: "Uh-oh. How am I going to make that team?" Montreal was coming off its sixteenth Stanley Cup Championship and the defense was packed with brilliant players — Serge Savard, Guy Lapointe, Jean-Claude Tremblay and Jacques Lapèrriere, just to name a few.

Larry went on to play in the minors for a season and a half. While with the Nova Scotia Voyageurs, Montreal's farm team in Halifax, Nova Scotia, Larry polished his skills and gained confidence. He toughened up and began to use his 6'4", 225-pound frame to intimidate opponents.

"When you get to live as many great moments as I have, all you can do is feel blessed to have been so lucky."

"Big Bird," as he was called, was eventually called up in the second half of the 1972–1973 season and never looked back. After starting the 1973 playoffs without a regular spot in the roster (and not dressing for some games), Larry worked hard and earned a regular place in the lineup. After just half a season with the team, he hoisted the Stanley Cup for the first time.

Larry went on to patrol the Montreal blueline for the next 16 seasons, helping Montreal win another five Cups. He was a part of what many believe was the finest defense ever — Montreal's "Big Three" which also included Savard and

Lapointe. He was most often partnered with Savard and the two complemented one another perfectly. Both were known mainly for their spectacular defensive abilities. Opponents likened facing Larry and Savard to "trying to skate through a pair of octopuses."

Larry left the Canadiens after the 1988–1989 season and signed with the Los Angeles Kings as a free agent. He played three seasons before retiring. He then coached in both L.A. and in New Jersey and won a Stanley Cup Championship with the Devils in 2000 as a head coach.

Larry also played in some memorable international games, including the New Year's Eve 1975 game between the Montreal Canadiens and the Soviet Red Army. Two of the best club teams in the world battled to a 3–3 tie in what is rated as one of the greatest games ever played. Larry also played for Canada in three Canada Cup tournaments in 1976, 1981 and 1984.

Larry was inducted into the Hall of Fame in 1995, and in November 2007 the Habs paid him the tribute of retiring his number 19.

Did You Know?

Remarkably, Larry never missed the playoffs during his entire career. Twenty seasons as an NHL player, 20 consecutive years in the playoffs. That's a boast no other player can make.

Born: June 2, 1951, in Winchester, Ontario
Position: Defence
Height: 1.93 m (6'4")
Weight: 102 kg (225 lbs.)
NHL Teams: Montreal Canadiens, Los Angeles Kings

CAREER STATS

Totals 1972–1973 to 1991–1992

	GP	G	A	PTS	PIM
Regular Season	1384	208	750	958	793
Playoffs	227	28	116	144	211
Major Awards	Stanley Cup Championship: 1973, 1976, 1977, 1978, 1979, 1986				
	Conn Smythe Trophy: 1978				
	James Norris Memorial Trophy: 1977, 1980				

BORJE SALMING

It's not uncommon today to see several players on an NHL team who were born outside of North America: think of Nicklas Lidstrom, Alex Ovechkin or Teemu Selanne. But back in the 1980s, almost every player in the league was born in Canada. It was Borje Salming, one of the greatest Swedish hockey players ever, who blazed the trail for great international players like Jari Kurri and Mats Sundin to play in the NHL.

Borje attracted the attention of a Toronto Maple Leafs scout in 1973 while playing in Sweden for Brynas IF Gavle. The scout thought he had dazzling puck-handling and skating skills and would have no trouble playing in the NHL.

"Every Swede respects Borje Salming and pays him tribute for what he has done. For us — Swedish hockey players — he is the man who showed us the right way. He is a trailblazer."

— fellow Swede and former Toronto Maple Leaf Mats Sundin

When Borje started playing in the NHL in 1973, his biggest challenge was to adjust to a much more physical style of play than he was used to. Skeptical fans and opponents expected Borje to prove himself. Rarely in the history of the NHL has one player taken so much physical and verbal abuse in his first season. He was run into the boards, hacked and challenged to fight by enforcers.

"There were lots of taunts of 'Chicken Swede.' There were threats to kill me. I heard every bad word there is," recalled Borje. "In the NHL they try to discourage you early. I got the same treatment and so does every rookie. If you fight back, they'll eventually leave you alone and let you play hockey."

Borje stood his ground and proved to be as tough, or tougher, than anyone else in the league. One example of his toughness and determination came in 1986. During a game in Detroit, Borje was knocked to the ice during a goalmouth scramble. While he was down, a Detroit player stepped on Borje's face and cut him. He received over 200 stitches. He was back in the lineup after just a few games.

Borje became a great player with some very good and very bad Toronto teams from 1973 until 1989. After 16 seasons, he left the Leafs to finish his NHL career with Detroit. "The King" left the Leafs as the team's top-scoring defenseman of all time and the all-time leader in career assists. Borje played another three seasons in Sweden before retiring at the age of 42. In 1996 he became the first Swedish-born player inducted into the Hockey Hall of Fame.

Did You Know?

During the 1976 Canada Cup tournament Borje was playing for Sweden against the U.S.A. at Maple Leaf Gardens in Toronto. When he was introduced before the start of the game, the fans gave one of the loudest, longest ovations the building had ever heard.

Born: April 17, 1951, in Kiruna, Sweden
Position: Defense
Height: 1.85 m (6'1")
Weight: 88 kg (193 lbs.)
NHL Teams: Toronto Maple Leafs, Detroit Red Wings

CAREER STATS

Totals 1973–1974 to 1989–1990

	GP	G	A	PTS	PIM
Regular Season	1148	150	637	787	1344
Playoffs	81	12	37	49	91

TERRY SAWCHUK

When Martin Brodeur recorded the 104th shutout of his career on December 21, 2009, he broke a record that had stood for more than 45 years. That record belonged to a man many feel was the greatest goalie to ever play the game: Terry Sawchuck.

Terry, who was nicknamed "Ukey" in reference to his Ukrainian heritage, started playing goal when he was around 10 years old. His coach sent letters to the Detroit Red Wings describing what a promising young goalie he was. When he was 14 years old the Red Wings brought him to Detroit so they could take a look for themselves. They couldn't believe their eyes. They knew this kid had an amazing future in hockey.

"His record speaks for itself. He's the best that ever played."

—former Toronto teammate Dave Keon

Terry finally got his chance with Detroit when their goalie was injured in 1949–1950. He filled in for seven games, but was impressive enough that Detroit traded their veteran away in the off-season. The next season, Terry played all 70 games, winning a league-leading 44 games and leading in shutouts with 11. It was no surprise when he was named NHL Rookie of the Year. Terry went on to lead the league in wins in each of the next four seasons — with Detroit winning the Stanley Cup three times.

Terry played the game with a ferocity few had ever seen, sacrificing every part of his body trying to stop the puck with very little padding. There weren't the synthetic, rock-hard materials that make up a goalie's armor today. One veteran reporter recalled seeing Terry in the dressing room one day and staring in disbelief "at the welts and bruises all over his body. It was a battlefield of blue, yellow and green welts and bruises."

Terry was traded to Boston for a couple of seasons before being traded back to Detroit, where he played another seven seasons before joining Toronto. He enjoyed three great years with the Maple Leafs and helped them to a Stanley Cup in 1967 before bouncing from Los Angeles to Detroit and then to the New York Rangers, where he played his final games.

Terry died at the age of 40 from injuries sustained during an off-ice fight with a teammate.

At the time Terry died he had more wins, more shutouts, had played in more games, and had won more Vezina Trophies than any other goalie in NHL history. He was inducted into the Hockey Hall of Fame in 1971.

Did You Know?
Terry started wearing a mask during the 1963 season after he was hit in the face by a Bobby Hull slapshot.

Born: December 28, 1929, in Winnipeg, Manitoba

Position: Goaltender

Height: 1.80 m (5'11")

Weight: 88 kg (195 lbs.)

NHL Teams: Detroit Red Wings, Toronto Maple Leafs, Los Angeles Kings, New York Rangers

CAREER STATS

Totals 1949–1950 to 1969–1970

	GP	W	L	T	SO	GAA
Regular Season	972	446	332	171	103	2.51
Playoffs	106	54	48	--	12	2.54

Major Awards	Stanley Cup Championship: 1952, 1954, 1955, 1967
	Calder Memorial Trophy: 1951
	Vezina Trophy: 1952, 1953, 1955, 1965
	Lester Patrick Trophy: 1971

EDDIE SHORE

Eddie Shore was a brilliant defenseman who dominated his position during the 1930s and was, at that time, the biggest star in the hockey world.

Eddie started his NHL career with the Boston Bruins in 1926. What made him dangerous was his ability to carry the puck deep into the offensive zone and either set up or score a goal. For a defenseman to do that at that time was unique. Eddie helped to make the Bruins one of the greatest teams of the era. They finished in first place in the American Division eight times in ten seasons and won the Stanley Cup in 1929 and 1939.

"I'm not sorry about anything I've ever done. As long as I'm close to hockey, I'm glad to be alive."

Eddie really developed during the 1932–1933 season. "The Edmonton Express" led all defensemen in scoring and was awarded the Hart Trophy as the NHL's Most Valuable Player. Eddie went on to win that award three more times — more than any other defenseman. Only Gordie Howe and Wayne Gretzky have won the Hart Trophy more often than Eddie.

Eddie was also known for his bad temper on the ice. During a tough game against the Toronto Maple Leafs on December 12, 1933, Eddie checked Toronto star Ace Bailey from behind. Bailey went into the boards headfirst and was nearly killed. The hit ended his career. Eddie always said that the hit was unintentional. When the first NHL All-Star Game was held as a benefit for Bailey the following season, Eddie and Bailey shook hands at center ice before the opening faceoff and received a standing ovation from the crowd at Maple Leaf Gardens.

In 1939 Eddie purchased a bankrupt minor league club in Springfield, Massachusetts. He split his time between Boston, playing in home games, and Springfield where he was managing his minor league club. The Bruins traded Eddie to the New York Americans and, for the rest of the season, he played 10 games for the Americans and another 15 for Springfield — where he also coached and managed!

Eddie was welcomed into the Hockey Hall of fame in 1947. He passed away in March of 1985 at the age of 82.

Did You Know?

In 1929 Eddie missed the team train to Montreal for a game against the Canadiens. Boston was experiencing one the worst snowstorms in years, but Eddie borrowed a car and convinced a driver to attempt the trip. Despite having to haul the car out of the ditch twice, Eddie made it in time for the game the next day.

Born: November 25, 1902, in
Fort Qu'Appelle, Saskatchewan
Position: Defense
Height: 1.80 m (5'11")
Weight: 86 kg (190 lbs.)
NHL Teams: Boston Bruins, New
York Americans

CAREER STATS

Totals 1926–1927 to 1939–1940

	GP	G	A	PTS	PIM
Regular Season	550	105	179	284	1047
Playoffs	55	6	13	19	181
Major Awards	Stanley Cup Championship: 1929, 1939				
	Hart Memorial Trophy: 1933, 1935, 1936, 1938				
	Lester Patrick Trophy: 1970				

PETER STASTNY

Peter Stastny's entry into the NHL was like a scene from an action movie: a car racing across the countryside, trying to stay one step ahead of the secret police, heading to the airport and freedom.

Back in the mid-1970s Peter was one of the greatest hockey players in the world. But he lived in what was then Czechoslovakia which was under communist rule. People were not allowed to leave the country to live elsewhere. If players were caught trying to defect, his career would be ruined. Most athletes didn't even try to leave. However, Peter wanted more. He wanted a chance to play the game he loved in the best league in the world.

> "I was very fortunate to achieve a number of team, and individual, accomplishments. To do it, one needed the good fortune of being surrounded and influenced by the right people. In this department, I was abundantly blessed."

Peter and his brother Marian grabbed the attention of the hockey world in 1976 on very powerful Czechoslovakian teams at the World Championship and the Canada Cup. Peter and Marian were joined by their younger brother Anton at the Olympics in Lake Placid in 1980. Peter led the team with 14 points in seven games. Not long after the Olympics, Peter and Anton decided to defect. Peter, his pregnant wife Darina, and Anton sped across the Austrian countryside in a car toward the airport in Vienna with Quebec Nordiques owner Marcel Aubut.

Aubut had arranged for the brothers to defect, and signed them both to six-year contracts.

Peter took to the NHL immediately, picking up 39 goals and 109 points and winning the Calder Trophy as Rookie of the Year. Peter particularly enjoyed the challenge of playing on the smaller North American ice surface.

"I found that the small ice made for a more physical game, but I liked it. I could take a hit and keep the puck and make one good move and get a scoring chance."

Peter went on to play 10 seasons with the Nordiques. He hit the 100-point mark in each of his first six seasons with the team. He ended his career having reached 100 points or more in a season seven times. He also finished in the NHL top ten scorers six times. Peter, a center, played in the same era as two of the greatest centermen in the history of the game — Wayne Gretzky and Mario Lemieux — so his accomplishments were often overlooked. He was traded to New Jersey in 1990 and was with the Devils for three seasons before finishing his NHL career in St. Louis. Peter has been inducted into both the Hockey Hall of Fame and the International Ice Hockey Federation Hall of Fame.

Did You Know?

During the 1980s, only Wayne Gretzky scored more points than Peter's 1,059.

Born: September 18, 1956, in
Bratislava, Czechoslovakia
(now Slovakia)
Position: Center
Height: 1.85 m (6'1")
Weight: 91 kg (200 lbs.)
NHL Teams: Quebec Nordiques,
New Jersey Devils, St. Louis Blues

CAREER STATS

Totals 1980–1981 to 1994–1995

	GP	G	A	PTS	PIM
Regular Season	977	450	789	1239	824
Playoffs	93	33	72	105	123
Major Awards	Calder Memorial Trophy: 1981				

BRYAN TROTTIER

All of the great NHL dynasties had great leaders — often more than just one. The 1970s Montreal Canadiens had Yvan Cournoyer and Guy Lafleur; the great Edmonton Oilers teams of the 1980s had Wayne Gretzky and Mark Messier. The New York Islanders were no different: with Bryan Trottier as one of their leaders, they went on to win four straight Stanley Cups.

"A quick message to all the youngsters out there: if you practice with emotion and purpose, you'll play with passion and confidence."

—Trottier, during his Hall of Fame induction speech

Bryan was a gritty, hard-nosed centerman who was just as likely to shut down the other team's best player as he was to score a hat trick. He spent 15 seasons with the Islanders and, aside from being part of those four Stanley Cup Championships, also won the Calder Trophy as NHL Rookie of the Year, the NHL scoring title, the Hart Trophy as the league MVP and the Conn Smythe Trophy as the playoff MVP.

To most hockey fans of that era, Bryan will always be linked to the players he spent most of his career playing on the same line with: Clark Gillies and Mike Bossy. The three were one of the greatest lines in NHL history. Gillies had great size and strength; Bossy had an amazing scoring touch; Trottier was one of the best passers in the game. Bossy and Bryan had great chemistry between them,

always seeming to sense where the other was on the ice.

"We had great communication between us," said Bossy years later. "We were never afraid to tell one another anything that we thought could help us to be better."

Unfortunately, Bryan's point totals started to drop off dramatically. He went from 82 points in the 1987–1988 season to 45 points the next. Things didn't get any better the season after that and Bryan, perhaps sensing that a change might help, left the Isles and signed with Pittsburgh as a free agent for the 1990–1991 season. He took on the role of mentor and unofficial coach to some of the younger players on the Penguins and was a big part of their back-to-back Cups in 1991 and 1992.

He retired for one season — working as an assistant coach with the Islanders — before returning to the Penguins in 1993 as a playing assistant coach. He retired at the end of that season and made the full-time transition to coaching.

Bryan, a six-time Stanley Cup Champion, was inducted into the Hall of Fame in 1997.

Did You Know?

Bryan holds the NHL record for most consecutive playoff games with at least one point. He scored points in 27 consecutive games in a streak in the 1980, 1981 and 1982 playoffs.

Born: July 17, 1956, in Val Marie, Saskatchewan

Position: Center

Height: 1.80 m (5'11")

Weight: 88 kg (195 lbs.)

NHL Teams: New York Islanders, Pittsburgh Penguins

CAREER STATS

Totals 1975–1976 to 1993–1994

	GP	G	A	PTS	PIM
Regular Season	1279	524	901	1425	912
Playoffs	221	71	113	184	277
Major Awards	Stanley Cup: 1980, 1981, 1982, 1983, 1991, 1992				
	Art Ross Trophy: 1979				
	Calder Memorial Trophy: 1976				
	Hart Memorial Trophy: 1979				
	Conn Smythe Trophy: 1980				
	King Clancy Memorial Trophy: 1989				

GEORGES VEZINA

The trophy awarded annually to the NHL's best goaltender is named after a man who played the game almost 100 years ago.

Georges Vezina learned to play goal on the streets of Chicoutimi, but didn't learn to skate until he was 16 and joined a local men's team. By 1909 he was playing for the Chicoutimi Saugueneens and, in an exhibition game against the Montreal Canadiens, led his team to an 11–5 win. The surprised Montreal manager quickly offered Georges a tryout. He made the team and signed a contract for $800. He played his first game for the Montreal Canadiens on the opening night of the 1910–1911 season.

> **"He stood upright in the net and scarcely ever left his feet; he simply played all of his shots in a standing position . . . I also remember him as the coolest man I ever saw, absolutely imperturbable."**
>
> **— former NHLer Frank Boucher**

Georges was one of the great stars in the National Hockey Association — the predecessor to the NHL — regularly leading the league in wins and fewest goals against.

Georges won his first of two Stanley Cup Championships in 1916. Back then the Cup wasn't an NHL-only competition. Montreal played a team from the Pacific Coast Hockey Association (the Portland Rosebuds) in a best-of-five series, which the Habs won. The Stanley Cup title was the first in Canadiens franchise history.

Georges' career had a sad and sudden end to it. Reports say that he showed up at training camp in 1925 looking thin and unhealthy and running a slight fever. His condition didn't improve much in the next few weeks, but he still managed to start Montreal's opening game on November 28. He left the game after the first period, but returned in the second before collapsing and being helped from the ice. Georges was diagnosed with tuberculosis, a severe infectious disease of the lungs, and died on March 27, 1926. Over a thousand people packed into a local church for his funeral and, before the start of the 1926–1927 season, the owners of the Canadiens donated a trophy named after their former star to be presented annually to the league's best goaltender.

Georges was inducted as one of the original 12 members of the Hockey Hall of Fame in 1945.

Did You Know?

From the time he signed with Montreal in 1910, right up until he had to leave his final game in November of 1926, Georges played every single game for the Canadiens — 325 consecutive games.

Born: January 21, 1887, in
Chicoutimi, Quebec
Position: Goaltender
Height: 1.68 m (5'6")
Weight: 84 kg (185 lbs.)
NHL Teams: Montreal Canadiens

CAREER STATS

NHA Totals 1910–1911 to 1916–1917

	GP	W	L	T	SO	GAA
Regular Season	138	72	65	1	2	3.61
Playoffs	13	6	7	--	1	4.36

NHL Totals 1917–1918 to 1925–1926

	GP	W	L	T	SO	GAA
Regular Season	190	103	81	5	13	3.28
Playoffs	13	9	4	1	2	2.77

Major Awards   Stanley Cup Championship: 1916, 1924

STEVE YZERMAN

Steve Yzerman made a name for himself in the Ontario Hockey League — one of the best junior leagues in the world — when he was just 16 years old. He started his hockey career as an offensive player, but later became more of a checking forward. His ability to adapt to situations around him didn't stop after his playing career ended, as he made the transition from superstar player to general manager in a very short time.

> "I've enjoyed every aspect. My whole career has really been a highlight in that I've really enjoyed playing. At the age of five, and before that, I really wanted to be an NHL player. It's all I ever wanted to do."

Those who watched "Stevie Y" play with the Peterborough Petes recognized his offensive talent; tape-to-tape passes and dazzling dekes brought fans out from around the league to watch him play. After two years with Peterborough, Steve was the Detroit Red Wings' 1st pick (4th overall) in the 1983 NHL Entry Draft. His timing couldn't have been better: the Red Wings were coming off some horrible seasons and had a new general manager who wanted to rebuild through the draft. Steve earned a spot in the lineup at just 18 years old. Then, entering his 4th NHL season, he was named captain of the Red Wings.

"I wanted a guy with a Red Wing printed on his heart," said his coach at the time, Jacques Demers, when he named Steve the youngest captain in the 62-year history of the franchise.

As captain, Steve accepted the Stanley Cup in 1997 — the first time the Wings had won it since 1955.

Steve scored a lot of points, particularly in his early years with the Red Wings. From 1987–1988 through 1992–1993, he never failed to reach the 100-point mark, averaging 122 points per season. He led the Red Wings in scoring for seven straight seasons. Later in his career, Stevie Y transitioned into one of the game's best defensive players. He won the Frank J. Selke Trophy as the NHL's Top Defensive Forward in 2000.

Aside from brilliance with Detroit, Steve was also a great contributor for Canada in the World Championships, the Canada Cup, World Cup and the Olympics, winning Olympic gold in 2002. After his retirement, Steve worked with Hockey Canada as a general manager and was the executive director of Canada's Olympic Team for the 2010 Vancouver Olympics. A few months later he was hired as general manager of the Tampa Bay Lightning.

Steve was officially inducted into the Hockey Hall of Fame in 2010.

Did You Know?
As of 2011–2012, Steve holds the NHL record for having served the longest as the captain of an NHL team: 19 seasons and 1,303 games.

Born: May 9, 1965, in
Cranbrook, British Columbia
Position: Center
Height: 1.80 m (5'11")
Weight: 84 kg (185 lbs.)
NHL Teams: Detroit Red Wings

CAREER STATS

Totals 1983–1984 to 2005–2006

	GP	G	A	PTS	PIM
Regular Season	1514	692	1063	1755	924
Playoffs	196	70	115	185	84
Major Awards	Stanley Cup: 1997, 1998, 2002				
	Conn Smythe Trophy: 1998				
	Frank J. Selke Trophy: 2000				
	Lester B. Pearson Award: 1989				
	Lester Patrick Trophy: 2007				
	Bill Masterton Memorial Trophy: 2007				

MAJOR NHL TROPHIES AND AWARDS

Art Ross Trophy
Awarded to the player who leads the league in scoring points at the end of the regular season

Bill Masterton Memorial Trophy
Awarded to the National Hockey League player who best exemplifies the qualities of perseverance, sportsmanship, and dedication to hockey

Calder Memorial Trophy
Awarded to the player selected as the most proficient in his first year of competition in the National Hockey League

Conn Smythe Trophy
Awarded to the most valuable player for his team in the playoffs

Frank J. Selke Trophy
Awarded to the forward who
best excels in the defensive
aspects of the game

Hart Memorial Trophy
Awarded to the player judged to
be the most valuable to his team

James Norris Memorial Trophy
Awarded to the defense player who
demonstrates throughout the season the
greatest all-round ability in the position

King Clancy Memorial Award
Awarded to the player who best exemplifies
leadership qualities on and off the ice and
has made a noteworthy humanitarian
contribution in his community

Lady Byng Memorial Trophy
Awarded to the player adjudged to have
exhibited the best type of sportsmanship and
gentlemanly conduct combined with a high
standard of playing ability

Lester B. Patrick Trophy
Awarded for outstanding service to
hockey in the United States

**Ted Lindsay Award
(formerly the Lester B.
Pearson Award)**
Awarded to the most outstanding
player in the NHL

**Maurice "Rocket"
Richard Trophy**
Awarded to the National Hockey
League's top goal scorer

Vezina Tophy
Awarded to the goalkeeper adjudged
to be the best at this position

NHL RECORDS

MOST CAREER GAMES PLAYED (REGULAR SEASON)

Gordie Howe	1767
Mark Messier	1756
Ron Francis	1731
Mark Recchi*	1652
Chris Chelios	1651

MOST GOALS, SINGLE SEASON

Wayne Gretzky, 1981–1982	92
Wayne Gretzky, 1983–1984	87
Brett Hull, 1990–1991	86
Mario Lemieux, 1988–1989	85
Phil Esposito, 1970–1971/	76
Alexander Mogilny, 1992–1993	76

CAREER POINTS, CENTER

Wayne Gretzky	2857
Mark Messier	1887
Ron Francis	1798
Marcel Dionne	1771
Steve Yzerman	1755

CAREER POINTS, LEFT WING

Luc Robitaille	1394
John Bucyk	1369
Brendan Shanahan	1354
Dave Andreychuk	1338
Bobby Hull	1170

CAREER POINTS, RIGHT WING

Gordie Howe	1850
Jaromir Jagr	1599
Mark Recchi*	1533
Jari Kurri	1398
Brett Hull	1391

CAREER POINTS, DEFENSEMAN

Raymond Bourque	1579
Paul Coffey	1531
Al MacInnis	1274
Phil Housley	1232
Larry Murphy	1216

*active player

WHO ARE YOUR FUTURE ALL-TIME GREATS?

Center:

_____

_____

_____

_____

_____

_____

Defense:

_____

_____

_____

_____

_____

_____

Left Wing:

_____

_____

_____

_____

_____

Right Wing:

_____

_____

_____

_____

_____

Goal:

_____

_____

_____

_____

_____